Crow and Goat

by Marilee Robin Burton
illustrated by Len Epstein

Core Decodable 82

McGraw Hill Education

Bothell, WA • Chicago, IL • Columbus, OH • New York, NY

MHEonline.com

Send all inquiries to:
McGraw-Hill Education
8787 Orion Place
Columbus, OH 43240

ISBN: 978-0-02-132339-5
MHID: 0-02-132339-9

Printed in Canada.

9 10 11 12 KOD 24

Crow and Goat went to their boat.

Crow and Goat hoped to see their pal Toad.

"Let's go fast, not slow!" said Goat.

"We will go fast in this boat!" boasted Crow.

"Let the wind blow!" bellowed Goat.

"Here we go!" yelled Crow.

But the wind did not blow, and their boat did not go.

Their boat did not go fast or slow.

“This boat only floats,” mumbled Crow.
Goat groaned.

"The boat has no sail!" yelled Toad.
"I think we must row," moaned Goat.